MW01235779

DARING COURAGE

Olivia Curry

authorHOUSE®

AuthorHouse™
1663 Liberty Drive
Bloomington, IN 47403
www.authorhouse.com
Phone: 1-800-839-8640

First published by AuthorHouse 12/29/2009

ISBN: 978-1-4490-5552-3 (e)
ISBN: 978-1-4490-5551-6 (sc)

Library of Congress Control Number: 2009913003

Printed in the United States of America
Bloomington, Indiana

This book is printed on acid-free paper.

Dedication:

I dedicate this book to my father, Ollie Curry. I love you and I miss you. Rest in peace Daddy…

Acknowledgments:

My Lord and Savior Jesus Christ, without You, I am nothing.

My mother, JoAnn Curry. Thanks for always being my rock and for always believing in me. I owe you the world.

To the loves of my life, Jordyn & Camryn. You are mommy's everything.

To my big sister Regina, words cannot explain what you mean to me. Your wisdom, strength, and dedication have always helped me get through every situation that I have ever been faced with.

To my talented big brother Reggie, thanks for always supporting and spoiling me.

To Bre, thanks for believing in your auntie and always being one of my biggest fans.

A special thanks to the ladies and gentleman who allowed me to tell their stories. You are all truly blessed and highly favored.

To my pastor Reverend Myers, thanks for always touching my spirit with true words from God.

Thanks to my PP&S fan club. I love you all.

To April Reign, you have an amazing gift that can never be taken away from you. Thank you so much for all of your help and providing me with the perfect title. May your talents take you far in life.

To Chris and this unbreakable bond that we share.

Thanks to Peter, Jerome, Teddy, Farzan, Cardell, & Sascha for all of your contributions.

Chapter 1

Be Encouraged…

In this book, I will be breaking down several categories that I've come to know quite well. I'm here to keep it real, so let's converse. You will find several different stories of real women who have been through trials and tribulations and who have overcome the disadvantages thrown at us by life, men, society, our jobs, and even our families, but at the end of the day, we're still here. No weapons formed against us prospered, and hopefully, you can learn something from our true stories. We are your average everyday women who work and pay taxes just like everybody else. We're not perfect, but we consider ourselves blessed and you should too. Now, first and foremost, let me start out by saying, "Ladies, you don't have to be the victim." Whether you are a victim of domestic violence, a victim of society, a victim of yourself, or a victim in your relationship with your man, you can change all of that and not be the victim anymore. Now, I'm no saint by far, but I'm a work in progress, so bear with me.

I know that there is something in this book for every type of woman. Want to know if workplace romances really work? Or how to survive and overcome an abusive relationship? Or how to move on with your life after being raped or cheated on by your man? Do all men cheat? I have the insight on how a lot of men feel about cheating. Are you a dark-skinned woman wounded by a racist society within your own race? Every woman needs to know how to become a virtuous woman and find her calling. One of the many great things about the Lord is that he gave us all "free will," which allows us to choose our paths in life, and it's quite simple. Do what makes you happy. If you are involved with something or someone that is not making you happy, then you need to let it go. Let's face it — we've all been the victim of something or someone at some point in our lives, and it was by our own free will that we are not in that situation anymore.

I put my heart and soul into this and I believe that many will be touched by something said in this book. Every story that is told in this book is near and dear to me and these are by no means fabricated stories. They are real events that either happened to me or someone I know well. I will discuss topics from relationship advice to self-esteem building techniques to ways we women can take over the world. I'm also going to tell you the one thing that every woman must do in order to make your relationship really work if it's meant to be and how, at the end of the day, we will all be held accountable for all of our actions. Each one of us has that one thing that makes us special. And that's what you have to find within yourself. What is it about you that sets you above the rest? What makes you tick? For me, it was writing this book. I sat on this idea for three years and I procrastinated one year after the other. I even convinced myself that maybe this was just an idea that would never come to pass, but after I lost my father to an ongoing battle with cancer and gave birth to my second daughter, I told myself that it was time to move; it was time to make this dream a reality. Life is too short to put off your hopes, your goals, or your dreams. And for who? For what? You can be here today and gone by the end of the day. Don't you think it's time to move in your life? Time to get up and do something positive that is going to make a change in your life that can help you and help someone else? A virtuous woman is a woman of courage and strength. She's not afraid to stand alone. She is admired for her acts of bravery, but often misunderstood. Don't worry about people misunderstanding you; everyone has their own thing that makes them special, and with that, you should never let your disadvantages be your hindrance.

Chapter 2

This Too Shall Pass...

Ladies, we have got to stop being the playing hand for these men. Remember, men can't run these games on us all by themselves. They need us to participate, or else they wouldn't have a hand to deal. How many women out there have found yourselves in this dreadful situation with your man? You love him, he says he loves you, but in the back of your mind, something just doesn't seem right. Many women may call this feeling you get in the pit of your stomach a curse and some may call it a gift. Whether it is a curse or a gift, 99.9% of the time, what you are feeling deep down inside is real. Now, whether you choose to act on your gut feeling or ignore it is up to you, but you had better believe that there is something there. It's called your female intuition, and ladies, if you get nothing else from this book, please listen to yourself. Your gut instinct doesn't lie! Just be sure not to mistake your female intuition for paranoia due to low self-esteem.

My coworker told me this quote," The grass may look greener on the other side until you get over there and see that it's artificial turf." I thought about that and it's absolutely true. A man can look good all day, but if he isn't any good and he doesn't treat you right, then at the end of the day, he just looks good. He doesn't have anything to offer you because he doesn't know how to treat a good woman. And he probably never had to treat a woman well because his looks always got him what he wanted. Women, you have to realize that many men take advantage of women with low self-esteem. They thrive on women who are weak-minded. And until you build up the strength in your mind and use that strength that God gave all women, then there will continue to be a lot of women putting up with anything from these men because they don't feel like there is anything better out there. Don't start up something with some random guy when you know you are not mentally strong, because you are going to keep falling in the same trap. First, take some time to strengthen yourself all over, then pray, and wait to receive your man.

Ladies, you have to empower yourselves. Don't settle for an average life when you can have so much more. I graduated with plenty of girls who grew up in single parent homes who are now doctors and making wonderful lives for themselves. We have to start changing our way of thinking and this goes for everybody – not just women. Reprogram your mind to a more optimistic way of thinking. I always say this quote to myself, "Positivity equals power, and power equals success." And that's God's plan for all of us. He didn't want things to turn out the way they have in the world. We can have heaven here on earth if we set our minds to better things. If you start listening to that voice inside you that constantly tells you that something is not right, you won't be stuck in these bad relationships with men who clearly aren't looking for the same thing out of the relationship that you are. Your female intuition is not just there as a guide to tell you if your kids are up to something. It tells you when there is something going on; listen to it. When it comes to women, it can be quite simple. As I stated earlier, do what makes you happy. Let me break that down a little bit. I'm not telling you that if it makes you happy to go around slapping people, do it. But if it's right, have at it – whether it is a career choice or a relationship. If you know that you are not happy with it, don't do it. If that man is sorry and you would be better off without him, let him go. He's hindering your happiness. We have to stop crying to these men and asking them, "Why are you doing this to me?" He is not doing anything to you that you are not letting him do. If you don't put up with it, then it can't be done to you.

Have a "Plan B." Every woman needs a backup plan, and that refers to everything in life – whether it is your relationship, career, living arrangements, or even your childcare arrangements – because you could get thrown a curve ball and not know where to turn. It's not being pessimistic or expecting the worst, but you also have to be smart and there's nothing wrong with having a backup plan.

Hold yourselves accountable for setting and meeting your "Better Me" goals. You have the power to turn the whole situation around if you would just empower yourselves. I'll never forget when it was time to get another car after I had my second daughter. I knew the mustang wasn't going to cut it anymore, but I wasn't real big on cars, and the ones that I did like, I couldn't afford, so I prayed. Then, I took action. I got all three of my credit reports and disputed everything I could and had some things removed. I paid off doctors' bills and over a six-month period, I raised my credit score and I saved some money. Then, one day, I saw this bad black car fly passed me on the highway as I was going to pick up my daughter from daycare, and as soon as I saw it, I knew that I had found my car. I programmed my mind to thinking that it was already my car – after six months of being told what I could and could not afford and that I would have to look for something else and settle for a car that I would not be happy with (which would have ended up with me not wanting to pay on it). So I took it upon myself to search online for the car. I knew exactly what I wanted because I really prayed about this thing, and was very detailed with my request to the Lord. I wanted that Toyota Camry Sports Edition in a dark grey with the sunroof, navigation system, two pipes on the back, a spoiler, a sports kit, fog lights, and a black grill. The week before I was to return to work from maternity leave, I did an extended search online for that car, I typed "navigation system" in the additional features box with the price range I was looking for, and there she was. It was the only car that popped up, and as soon as I saw it, I knew that was my car. I wasn't worried about getting financed because I had already talked to Jesus about it and I knew he had my back. The next morning, I called the dealership and I told that car salesman that I was coming to get that car. I called the bank and got approved for the amount of the car. I then called my sister and told her, "I found my car! Want to go with me to pick it up?" Nothing ever came easy for me; the car was over 300 miles away, but that wasn't stopping me. So the next morning, me, my sister, my mom, and my two-year-old took a road trip in my mustang to go get my new ride. When we finally pulled up at the dealership, they had it sitting out front waiting on me. I'm here to tell you that was a wonderful feeling to be able to get that car and it was what I wanted and it was all because of the Lord. Now, my Camry SE might not be much to you, but it meant a lot to me because it was something I was able to do for myself. I didn't need a man to co-sign for me. My dad was no longer here to help. I didn't call on anybody but Jesus, and He delivered. You don't need a man to make things happen for you; it's so much better when you can do things for yourself, and men respect a woman who can hold her own and who is not always looking for a handout from them. Had I not had the faith, there is no telling what I would have ended up with. I used to see this car going down the highway every other day when I was picking my baby up from daycare and I would always say to myself, *I'm going to get that car.* That car had my name on it, and now, when I pass by that Camry on the highway, I smile because it's no longer a dream. I made it happen for myself and that is a great feeling.

Don't let a bad situation like a breakup keep you down. Use that as motivation to do better with your life. I know breakups can be devastating and sometimes it seems like it's going to take forever and a day for the pain you feel in your heart to go away, but I promise that if you pray a sincere prayer to the Lord and ask Him to strengthen you, He'll make everything alright. It doesn't matter what you look like; God made you and he didn't make any mistakes, so you are worth everything and you need to show that to yourself. Don't fall victim to yourself because then you will never be treated right by a man. You will always be taken advantage of and not just by him, but by society as well. Hold yourself to high standards. You need to take that breakup and turn it into a blessing. Follow these tips that I used.

1. **Start working out.** In these times, money is short, so take some time out of your day, whether it is thirty minutes or one hour, and go to a park and start walking. It's free and relaxing. If you have an MP3 player, put that on with some positive and inspiring music and walk it out. You'll be surprised at how much better you'll feel, emotionally and physically. I have recently had to do this.

2. **Read a book.** Joel Osteen has great motivational books that help you get through anything.

3. **Start hanging out with your friends more – your positive friends.** Even if you are going window-shopping, go with a girlfriend who's going to keep you laughing, because laughter is good for the soul. Join Face book and link up with old friends. It's free and you'd be surprised at how many people you know are joined as well.

4. **Go to church.** There's nothing like going to church and hearing some good singing and getting the word of God. And you don't have to limit yourself to just your church. Visit other churches. Go to a friend's church.

5. **Get a makeover.** Makeovers don't have to be expensive. Go get the latest haircut and spice up your wardrobe by catching the sales at your favorite store.

6. **Get rid of negative influences.** If it is someone in your life that never has anything positive to say and thrives off other people feeling bad, then you need to let them go. You'll feel ten times better if you surround yourself with positive people.

7. **Stop gossiping.** If you spent more time working on yourself and helping others than you spent trying to figure out who got into it at work, you would be a lot better in life.

8. **Take a trip**. Pick a nice place that you've always wanted to visit and start setting some money aside to get out of town.

9. **Start saving money and go back to school.** If you have a degree that you are not doing anything with, get a degree in something else. It's never too late to go back to school. Stop wasting time on situations that don't agree with the lifestyle that will make you happy.

10. And last but not least, **put yourself back on the market**. I'm not telling you to sleep around town, because that's not the answer. But after you've changed your wardrobe, and started implementing those positive things into your life, you will be able to find someone that you can have a nice conversation with or someone to take you out on a date from time to time. But I must

warn you that putting yourself back on the market can be more hurtful than helpful sometimes, because you could wind up talking to some jerk or going out with a complete looser who will only make you think that your ex wasn't so bad. Then, before you know it, you will find yourself back at point A. You have to know how to weed out the bad guys. Don't waste any more time trying to break in that man, because by the time you try to finish breaking him in, you'll be worn out. You have to understand that a man is not going to change until he is ready.

Once you reach a certain age, it's time to really put things into perspective, and if you haven't already, start making some lifelong decisions about your future. If you know you want to have kids someday, but the man you are after is either done having kids, doesn't like kids, or doesn't want any, you need to take that into consideration. It will become a major conflict of interest when you try to suppress your feelings for wanting children and he has no intentions of having children or he has no intentions of having children with you.

In closing for this lesson, please learn to have a mind of your own. Stop letting other people influence how you feel about another person because their perception of someone might be completely different than what you might see in that individual. I've seen people not like someone because of something they heard someone else say. I've said it before and I'll say it again, I'm no saint, but I do know that one day, we are all going to be held accountable for our actions, and if you are running around talking about how you can't stand somebody because of someone you know that doesn't like them, that's not good. I've been in this situation before, and it's not worth the wasted time and energy you are going to put into it.

Chapter 3

Workplace Romances: Do They Really Work?

I've heard all the gossip and personal remedies on this subject from a lot of people, and I've come to a conclusion through past experience with workplace romances: Somebody's going to have to find another job. Take it from me, it's good when it's good, but when things go south, the last thing the two of you need is to be at the same job at the same time. You may start out with tough skin, but I think it's healthier for a couple to be able to miss each other, and if you share the same job, the same household, and the same time and space outside of work, then you really don't have that time to miss one another. Don't get me wrong; I'm not saying that 100% of workplace romances fail, but I can tell you that there will be some sort of drama.

Don't believe me; check out this woman's workplace tragedies. You are probably thinking, *What do these women know? My boo is different.* But listen to this, women: The four times I tried it, I thought, *This is my boo, my man, my sweetie, and he is different,* too. It's not that they don't mean well, because I honestly think they go into things with good intentions. After it's all said and done, you end up either not speaking or you and he are doing little childish things to make the other jealous, and then you convince yourself that you are not really ready to let go because you have invested so much time and effort into the relationship. But ladies, I'm here to tell you, when they say never mix your money with your honey, trust me. It simply does not and will not work. Don't get me wrong; they start out so sweet, so attentive, so thoughtful, and yes, so giving. And I don't mean monetarily, even though they do that too, but I'm talking about giving themselves physically and emotionally.

In relationship one, this man made me feel like I was the most important lady in his life, next to his mother. I honestly felt that if he treated his mother well, then he would know how to take care of me as well. Wrong! It took several years and a child with him for me to realize that he was too much of a mama's boy to ever be a real man for me, and that was the least of his problems. Like I said, he had good intentions, but good intentions don't always lead to a "happy ever after."

We started out just going to eat breakfast together after our shift was over each day. He was always quick to drive and quick to pay for everything. Our first Valentine's Day, he came over before our night shift to bring me some candy and a stuffed animal. That made a good impression on my parents. The next month was my birthday, and he picked me up and took me to work. Then later, he took me out to dinner, to a movie, and he bought me an outfit. By this time, I had decided to give him some of my cookies. After we made love for the first time, we became inseparable. After all that quality time was spent, and after all the movies, dinners, and shopping, it turned out he was dating an older woman and (can you believe it?) they were engaged. Even though he left her for me, so he said, it still didn't work out. We still dated for two years and I let him convince me that we were going to get married and that we could go ahead and have a child. This is another mistake we make. Get married first! Don't let him convince you to have his child without first making it right. As it turns out, he was seeing another co-worker behind my back, which happened to be someone I knew. He was seen with a different woman in public and I felt so betrayed because I thought it was something everyone knew about but me. Once, at work, one chick walked by me and said the wrong thing on the wrong day, and before I knew anything, I had grabbed her.

Some of our co-workers grabbed me, and one of them said, "She ain't worth it and neither is he," and I let her go. I was actually about to lose my job over him playing mind games with me and these other women. Ladies, that's when you know you need to stop, because I could have jumped on that girl and lost my job and they would have still been messing around.

I guess I let him continue to live with me for our daughter's sake. This is another mistake. Don't try to make a bad relationship work just for the kids because it only makes it worse, especially when they see you arguing all the time. That is not a good environment for your kids.

One day, I asked my daughter how she would feel if daddy didn't live with us anymore. She was five at the time, but she knew what was going on. She said, "Mommy, will I still get to see my daddy?"

I said, "Of course; your daddy loves you. He will still get to spend time with you." And that was good enough for her. After that, I let him go. Our daughter is now a teenager and he still isn't married, and hell, neither am I for that matter, but we have a civil relationship. One thing I can say about him is at the end of the day, he always has my back. But if I hadn't changed jobs, I don't think we would have been able to maintain such a friendly relationship.

So after that workplace romance didn't work, I had to try it again. In relationship two, as I stated earlier, we sometimes date another co-worker in hopes of making our ex jealous – another big mistake. Hooking up with somebody on the rebound just to get back at somebody won't work; take it from me. But this guy was fine and he drove one of my favorite cars. We were hot and heavy for a while. It didn't take long for me to realize he just wanted someone to take care of him. I went all out for him for Christmas because I thought we were in a relationship. You know how it works . . . . You get him something, he gets you something, and so on. Well, let's just say ten plus years later, I still haven't received that Christmas gift he "forgot" to bring me. Even though the sex and the spontaneity were exciting, it didn't last very long. But it did make my now-Baby Daddy extremely jealous, at least for a little while. You know how it works . . . . They don't want you, but they don't want anybody else to have you either – selfish bastards. I guess I still never learned, because here I was again – different job and, sadly, another workplace romance.

This next guy was really a sweetie, but you know

there are always signs to let us know when things aren't quite right. You know that intuition thing we usually ignore? Well, first of all, we had a lot of the same interests. We both loved and drove Mustangs and he had a motorcycle, which was a big hook for me because I always wanted one. He was so thoughtful and was always coming up with things to do that he knew would make me happy. He loved going out to dinner and he would surprise me with overnight trips out of town. Sometimes, he would leave sweet notes on my car, and sometimes, he would tell me to leave my car unlocked and he would leave the itinerary for a special night that he would have planned for us at a nice hotel. We always stayed at hotels with Jacuzzi tubs and he would spoil me with massages. He always brought me lunch at work. I just enjoyed being with him. And he made me feel like he enjoyed my company as well. But as time went by, I realized that he never invited me to anything dealing with his family (hint hint) – no birthday parties, no cookouts. He actually never mentioned those things until after the fact. I knew that he didn't want me to meet his family for some reason. It wasn't until later that I found out he had a little boy and apparently he was still dealing with his baby momma because she was pregnant with his twins. He never mentioned anything to me about her or them for that matter. It just so happened that one of my girlfriends from work got a cigar from his dad because he was passing them out to celebrate his new twin granddaughters. That just put a damper on the whole thing; I was devastated. Of course, he tried to make it seem so trivial, but I couldn't get past it. After him, I swore to myself that I was done with the workplace romances because I couldn't even stand the sight of him at work after that. But that too was short lived.

I had found myself in a situation I really did not want to be in, but when it came to this guy, I couldn't help it. This man took the whole cake. We worked on the same shift. He was a little bit older than I was, and did I mention that he was MARRIED? The biggest no-no of them all! I must say, regrettably, that he was the best out of them all. I know people say this a lot, but it wasn't anything planned; it just happened. I knew better because I had been there and done that so many times before, just not with a married man. This man was everything I ever wanted. He too had a fascination with motorcycles and he too loved to travel. He was tall, handsome, and athletic from playing football. He made me feel so secure when I was with him – so much so that I almost convinced myself that we had something special and that he was mine. We did almost everything together. We went to dinner, of course, we went out of town, we went shopping, he took care of things around my house, he helped me pay my bills, he would plan trips with my daughter and me – another big no-no, but I'll talk about that in a second. He was there for me emotionally and physically. The man had it going on. We had become so involved with each other that he got his own place just to make my daughter think we were a real couple. He had become so attached to her that he said that he wouldn't do anything to make me or her upset with him. He started staying at my house more than he stayed at home and we were always at his place. He even gave me a key. I think I would still be in that situation had it not been for my conscience and that feeling of guilt I would get every time I prayed. Lord knows I have always longed to be married to a man that would love and respect both me and my daughter, but I knew in my heart that God would not take someone else's husband from them and give him to me. But when you are all involved in that type of situation, the devil will make you think so. Since I have gotten more involved with church and reading the bible, I have really been working on myself spiritually. I know that God has a husband out there just for me. And this last time, I truly thought I had found the one.

Here I was again, new job, same story. But somehow, this time, it felt different. I met this guy through a mutual co-worker. And let's just say the first night that I saw him, our eyes met at the same time and I swear there was an automatic attraction. He came straight over to where my friend and I were sitting and he started asking me questions. It was such an intense connection that my friend moved to another table to give us some space to talk. I felt an immediate closeness to him. But like I said earlier, the devil is always busy and he's good at making you think everything is okay and then pulling the rug up from under you. But it was something about this man. I don't know what it was, but it made me feel like this was the one, like we just belonged together. The more we talked, the more we found out we had in common. And, oh yeah, he was a member of a bike club too! I thought, *This is for me.* I was finally going to beat this workplace romance myth. He loved the finer things in life – the best restaurants, hotels, and stores. Do you see a pattern here? We both loved to go to football games; you name it, we both loved it. I introduced him to my family and they hit it off as well. He took me to his parents' house and I had a good time as well. Things were really good between us for a while, until . . .

He became so busy with his own business and he was starting a new one, not to mention the job that he had at the same place at which I worked. I was busy with school and some family problems came up that caused us not to be able to spend any time together. That's when the real him showed up. We had been talking to each other off and on and trying to see each other whenever we could steal a moment or two. But with everything going on, it was still good to have someone to talk to, someone who I felt was still there for me.

One day at work, another co-worker and I were leaving the break room and we overheard another woman talking about this man. She went on to say that she was in love with this man who just so happened to have the same name as my man. The more she described him, the more I knew that she was talking about him. I couldn't believe it! I felt like I had been kicked in the gut and the wind was knocked out of me. She didn't seem to have any idea about me and him because he worked nights and I was on days. I was also very adamant about keeping our relationship on the low low. Of course, you know he denied everything, but I knew that with all that stuff I had heard that day, that either she was delusional or he was lying and it didn't take me long to figure out that he was lying. The Lord just put me in the right place at the right time to hear what I needed to hear. To make a long story short, this man had been around the block at work and I was just one of his many conquests. The fact that he looked like Morris Chestnut made him the man when he first got there. You know, a man can be so smooth with his words and actions that you never see or hear anything. And that's how it was with me until that particular day when I heard everything. One of the same chicks that my ex from another job was sleeping with, she now works at the same place with me again and of course, she was with my man here too. But that's another story.

Even now, to this day, he declares he loves me and will win me back somehow. I must honestly say that during my celibacy, I have almost been drawn back in by his sweet words and his beautiful smile. But when I get to work and see all those other conquests of his, and there were many, it really snaps me back into place. I have realized that if someone loves you, they definitely wouldn't do anything to hurt you. The fact that he did it right there under my nose just reiterates what this chapter is all about. Workplace relationships simply do not work, and at the end of the day, you can't just quit your job when things don't work out. So ladies believe me when I tell you to not mix your money with your honey.

As I stated earlier, I believe that God has a husband just for me and he has one for you too if only you would be patient, do the right thing, and start getting yourself ready for him. I know I may not find him when I'm looking for him, when I want him, or on my own timetable, but I know he's out there, and I pray every day for the knowledge and understanding to be able to recognize him when he comes and you should pray that prayer too. In addition, I believe with every fiber of my being that he's not in our workplace, because professionally, we're not where we want or need to be yet.

Now, back to me. On the other side of town, at a completely different place of business, I was going through something similar, but what I was dealing with went a lot deeper than I can even explain. I'm not the type who likes to keep drama stirring and you won't find me gossiping about everyone in the building. I had gotten to the point where I just wanted people to stay out of my relationship, but after the constant attempts, of course it took its toll on me. The old Olivia who didn't have kids would have made an example of somebody, but as I stated earlier, they are simply not worth it and I'm much more mature than that now. Just like the story above, I had a child by the man who was my honey at the time. We had been on and off for some years and I thought that after all the breakups and makeups, we were still meant to be together. I put up with all the childish women – showing up at his desk, walking by my desk, leaving cards on his desk, trying to flaunt by his desk, calling his desk. You name it, they did it. I mean, they took persistence to a whole other level. It was pathetic. I didn't know that females over the age of 18 could act so simple and scandalous, but immaturity and stupidity has no age limit. As I stated earlier, you know it's time to stop when you get to the point when you're about to have a physical altercation with one of the women, because you don't need to stoop to her level because she's definitely not worth losing your job over.

I had to take a look at the picture of my kids on my desk and send a quick prayer up to the Lord just to help me make it through the work day. But I'm here to tell you, once I started praying more and reading my bible, the Lord lifted all those negative situations and turned them into something positive. There will always be someone out there that always wants what the next person has. They fall into the same category as haters.

Most of the time, as women, we tend to put it all on the other women, but you have to remember that there is a man who is allowing all these things to take place. A man who has the utmost respect for his relationship and his woman would shut down any disrespectful acts from another woman and he would do it without hesitation. Ladies, you shouldn't have to be the one to put these chicks in their place. They only keep at it because it's being entertained, but I'll go into more detail on that in a later chapter. Just remember, before you do something stupid that could cause you to lose your job, think about the bigger picture and the fact that you could lose much more than you will gain by acting out of anger at work. You have to learn to be the smarter, bigger woman. Nine times out of ten, the women who are working hard at your relationship failing are already known for wrecking homes. The funny thing is, they like to play the victim, like someone is out to get them, but I don't know of any real woman who goes around saying, "I want to be a home wrecker just like her." Any woman who has respect for herself and any values or morals would not be hounding after another woman's man. I've seen and heard it all – the girls that speak and give little compliments that mean nothing and then turn around and send texts to your man. They look at the car, the clothes, the money they think he has, and (this is one that gets me) the hair – all of the material things that do not make a relationship. But remember, it's not really about you. They couldn't care less about you. It's about your man. And if they get the chance to sleep with him, they will. Why are women scandalous? That plagues me the most. Whatever happened to being happy for one another and going out and trying to find your own happiness? Only in a perfect world, I guess.

To sum up the whole workplace romance dilemma, it is the lack of people minding their own business. Stop sitting around at work waiting to hear about the next person's business and trying to find out what's going on in someone else's relationship. You know, the problem with the world today is everybody is minding somebody else's business. I mean, think about it. If Bush wouldn't have been minding Iraq's business, we wouldn't have lost thousands of troops in the wrong country. We should have minded our own business and left Iraq alone. They didn't have anything to do with us directly, but again, this is just my opinion and I'm entitled to it. Now, Bin Laden is another story. If he would have been minding his own business in Afghanistan, we wouldn't have to be over there playing hide and seek with him and losing more of our troops today, but that's a completely different story.

The bottom line is dating a co-worker has it's positives and negatives, as does everything in life. Just be careful and know what you are getting yourself into. Everything is all good as long as you are getting along, but as soon as things go south, there will be drama. You won't be able to stand the sight of each other and it will be hard to try to put on a happy face when your relationship is falling apart. By this time, everyone will know, and they are like predators – at the first sign of trouble, they go for the kill. We are not banning the idea of workplace romances; we are just giving you the heads up.

Courage
The rage within to persevere anyway
Past fear, doubt, and hopelessness To dream in
darkness

Stephanie Captain

Chapter 4

Be Grateful For Your Haters

My friend Meka once told me to think of haters as your fans. They act just like fans – they want to be like you, they want to have what you have, and they want to find out as much about you as possible. The more I thought about it, the more it made sense, because that's exactly what haters do. I'll never forget the time right before I started middle school when my sister pulled me to the side one day and told me that a lot of things were about to change for me. She said, "People that you thought were your friends will turn their backs on you and talk about you." She told me that a lot of girls who didn't even know me were not going to like me. I didn't really know what she was talking about until I started school my sixth grade year and I'll never forget it. I had started cheerleading when I was in elementary school, and when I got to middle school, I tried out for the team, and I made it. I have always had an outgoing personality and I always have a smile on my face. I was the easygoing cool girl who liked to have fun, but just as my sister had warned me, I gained some enemies. Girls that didn't even know me were giving me mean looks and trying to start fights with me. I couldn't figure out why, but my sister told me that they were just jealous of me and that they just wanted to be like me. That same scenario followed me all through high school. I was involved in everything that went on in school. I was class president, in student council, a varsity cheerleader, in homecoming, and involved in pageants. You name it; I did it. But none of that stuff made me treat people any differently. I was still that same cool girl who spoke to everybody and kept that smile on my face. I never let any of that stuff go to my head and I'm still that way to this day because that's how I was raised. But not everybody looked at it that way; some of the friends I had leaving middle school were not my friends leaving high school, especially when it came to boys. I learned that the quickest way to end a friendship with a girl is to bring a male into the equation. I saw more friendships end over boys than anything else. The sad thing is that rule still stands today for grown women. There are more grown women right now who aren't speaking because of a man. This whole "haters" reality can be broken up into several different categories, but I guarantee you that over 80% of it is geared towards someone of the opposite sex. A man will hate on another man because he wants what that man has, and most of the time, it's his woman. A woman will hate on another woman because she doesn't have a man and wants hers or she just wants a man and is mad at her because she has one.

I said "hater" reality earlier because it's far from a theory; it still exists just like racism. I mean, think about it. Of course, there will be haters. This world is built around people hating on each other. Take Jesus, for example. Jesus was perfect and could do no wrong and he had haters. Look at the Pharisees. They hated Jesus, which tells us that "The Hater" has been around since the biblical days. So what would make you think that everyday sinners aren't running around getting kicks out of somebody else's pain? Which brings me to my next reason why there are haters. My pastor always says that people don't mind you getting ahead, as long as you don't get ahead of them. And that was one of the realest statements I've ever heard. There are people out there with degrees who have envious personalities. It's easier to spot a hater out of a crowd of people than any other type of human being. They are everywhere. Ladies, don't be fooled by these women who smile in your face and speak to you every day like you are all cool, because the second you turn the corner, they are whispering and spreading gossip. To be able to deal with a hater, you have to understand what a hater's role is. First, they have to investigate. They want to find out everything they can about you from other people. They end up knowing more about your business than you do. But at the end of the day, just let haters do their job and don't worry about them. I'm here to tell you, there is no need to worry, because just as they are trying to bring you down, the Lord will lift you up. You need to follow that old saying "kill them with kindness" and walk around with an 'S' on your chest and God by your side. Who can defeat that? Let them hate. At least you know you are special enough for someone to be one of your fans. I had a woman at one of my jobs who did everything she could to try to get to me. She would try to associate herself with anyone she knew who was close to me.

You have to treat childish women the same way you treat haters. Nine times out of ten, these people have some insecurity that they are trying to cover up by putting someone else down. It may sound ridiculous, but you will be surprised at the number of childish women in their mid to late twenties, thirties, and even forties. Immaturity doesn't discriminate based on age. There are childish women everywhere, and how you handle them makes all the difference, because they are just like haters – here to stay. Since I started back working in the civilian world, I have run into some of the most immature so-called 'grown' women that I have ever seen in my life. I was in the military for six years and I never had the childish dealings with female soldiers I have had with civilian women. It's like two completely different worlds. But the way to deal with them is simple. It's not by following them up, but by praying for them. I promise; it works. I've had to name a few of them individually in prayer and ask the Lord to deal with them and hold on to me just to keep me from setting it off on them.

I went to a church service in Thomson, Georgia, and the preacher was a young guy in his twenties who preached like he had been doing it for years, and he preached as if he were speaking directly to me. He talked about how to defeat your enemies by making them your bread makers and he described it by saying "your enemy is going to write your check." And what I got from his sermon is that as long as you handle things in a Godly manner and let Him fight your battles for you, He will make your enemy your footstool to spiritual success. You can't do that by gossiping to any and everybody about people and trying to get even with them for the wrong things that they have done to you. And that's what I had been doing, but I realized that it didn't make them go away, so I prayed. Months later, back at my home church, we had our annual revival services where the Reverend James Hall was the guest speaker for the week. He spoke on the topic of defeating your enemies too, and he said that instead of talking bad about your enemy to someone else, talk to Jesus. Tell him all about it. Don't bring yourself down to the level of your enemy because then you are no better than they are. He preached from the book of 1 Samuel, and it discusses the people appointing Saul as King over Israel, which was not the king that the Lord wanted, and after He rejected Saul, the Lord sent Samuel to Jesse's house, where He appointed David as the new king over Israel. When the Israelites went to battle with the Philistines, there was a champion named Goliath, who, according to the bible, stood over nine feet tall. Goliath was challenging any man of Israel to come and fight him one on one. Now, Saul was still king at the time because David had not been anointed yet and everyone in Saul's camp, including Saul, was afraid to go and face Goliath, but not David. He approached Saul and told him that he would go and kill Goliath and since there was no one else who was brave enough to fight, Saul sent David. As he approached Goliath, he looked at David as if he were a joke. *Who dared send this boy to battle me?* He thought.

And David said to Goliath, "I come against you in the name of the Lord Almighty, the God of the armies of Israel, whom you have defied." In the end,

31

David defeated Goliath by shooting a stone from his slingshot, hitting Goliath in his forehead, and Goliath fell to his death. Then, David took Goliath's sword, stood over him, and cut his head off. And that, my friends, is how you defeat your enemy. David didn't need any fancy armor, but because he believed and had faith in the Lord, his enemy was defeated. And that's what we must do. Destroy our enemies in the name of God. But we must remember that with any great triumph, there will be jealousy, because even after David defeated Goliath, Saul became jealous of him. He made several attempts to kill David, and it was Saul that fell on his own sword, killing himself. The lesson learned from this story is that no matter how many times your enemies attack you, eventually, they will lose at their own game.

I believe what it says in the bible – no weapons formed against me shall prosper because no matter how hard they tried, they could not get me down. Yes, the roads were rough, and I'm not perfect, because there were times when I felt like it would have been easier to just curse them out and tell all of their business. But it wasn't the right thing to do.

There was a quote on the front of our programs for revival that week and it said, 'Every Saint Has a Past, Every Sinner Has a Future' and that is true. I can honestly say that I left revival a better person. I gave up a lot of my childish ways and I had to remember that I too had a past that I was not proud of and that before I could spread things about someone else, whether they had done me wrong or not, I knew from where the Lord had brought me. I have said it before and I'll say it again – I'm not perfect and I'm still a work in progress, but I am nothing like I used to be. My pastor Reverend Myers talks about that a lot at church too, and the truth is that everyone has a past and everybody has a story of how they got over it. So I changed my tactics – no more trying to bring my enemies down my way. I turned to the Lord. Let's all take steps to better our lives together.

Chapter 5

Dark-skinned Racism

I was brought to tears when I watched an episode of the *The Tyra Banks Show* about dark-skinned women. When I heard how some women said they were teased just because they were dark-skinned, it saddened me, because it was coming from adults. Of course, in elementary school, kids tease all the time, but some of these women were actually mistreated by their own families because they were the darker child. I couldn't believe some of the drastic measures some women would take just to look like somebody other than the person God made them. I mean, some of these women actually bleached their skin to make themselves look lighter. Ladies, it is not that serious. I've never been turned down for a job because I was dark-skinned, because every job that I really wanted, I got. But it doesn't stop there. On another episode of *The Tyra Show*, there was a black homosexual male who discriminated against other black men that were darker than he was. Isn't that one of the biggest double standards you have ever heard of? There is a difference between preferring to date someone of a certain complexion and hating someone who has a skin tone that is darker than yours. That's just ridiculous.

I'm here to tell you that we dark-skinned women

are some of the world's most beautiful women I have ever seen and dark-skinned men are simply gorgeous and you should not let anyone make you feel bad about the way God made you. But why is it that you don't see many dark-skinned couples together? You either see a lighter complected male with a dark-skinned women or vice versa. I think it's the "opposites attract" theory. You would be surprised at the number of women who are threatened by beautiful dark-skinned women. Let's be honest here. Yes, black is beautiful and black is back, baby. If you think you need to have a lighter complexion just to get a man to look at you, then you need to relocate because there are plenty of men out there that want nothing more than a beautiful chocolate confident woman by their sides. Notice I said confident, because you don't want a man with you who knows that your self-esteem is so low that he talks to you only because he feels sorry for you. When you walk in a room, you shouldn't be sizing everyone up in the room by who is dark-skinned or light-skinned, white or black. Just walk in the room and own it. You have to change your way of thinking about this whole thing or you will always be the victim. Some of us become victims of ourselves and that's the worst kind of problem. I don't hate on women that are lighter than I am, nor do I pay that any attention. At the end of the day, aren't we all women of God? I wouldn't want to have any other complexion. There are enough skin types and tones to go around for everyone and we were not made to all look alike, so take pride in your beautiful, glowing skin. Don't let the whole media and music world put you down because you are darker. We are still living in a racist world and the bad part about it is the racism is within our own race.

I was watching videos with my mom one day and she said, "Where are the dark-skinned girls?" And when I really paid attention to it, she was right. Think about it. Who do you see on all the hip hop music videos? You might see one dark-skinned girl every five videos. It's like we are uncommon or something. But let me tell you, baby, we might be rare and uncommon to them, but we are unique. Let me just say that, yes, everyone's entitled to their own opinion and preference regarding who they like. But there are a lot of beautiful dark-skinned women out there, and for once, I would like to see a variety of women on these videos and in magazines – not just the average look of the lighter complected women. Yes, they are beautiful too, but they do not represent the only complexion there is.

Dark-skinned people have evenly toned skin. Most people have to apply some sort of beauty product to make their skin evenly toned. I never wear foundation or any kind of heavy makeup on my face and I don't have to. I do my eyes and my lips and that's all you're going to get out of me. I have used Bare Minerals, which is an all-natural product that doesn't leave your face looking like you have a bunch of clay caked up on your face. This product enhances your already dark and lovely glow.

I remember one time I was going into Hamrick's and I saw this guy driving by. Now, this man was looking and leaning so hard that he almost fell out of the car. Needless to say, he got out. Here he comes in the store, just staring at me, and I got this smirk on my face because I was trying not to laugh. Now, I had my little girl with me and she was sitting in the buggy playing when he walked up.

"I'm sorry to bother you, but you are the prettiest dark-skinned woman I have ever seen and I wanted to know if you had a man?" he said.

"Yeah, I'm taken, but thanks," I said, and started to walk off.

Then, he goes, "Is he treating you right?"

"Yes he is. Have a good day."

Then, he finally went the other way. Then, I got to thinking, why do men say you are pretty for a dark-skinned girl. Like, if you are dark-skinned, they automatically expect you to be ugly. I mean, some people act like it's a privilege to be an attractive dark-skinned woman. Why is it that we are racist within our own race? I hear other light-skinned black men and black women talking about dark-skinned women as if they are better than we are. We have become so divided as a people that we are broken up into categories: high yellow, red, brown skin. I've even heard women refer to themselves as bronze or ebony. Whatever happened to just being black? Did you know that back in the day, some grandparents treated their own grandchildren differently according to the complexion of their skin? The lighter kids would get more to eat than the darker kids. I'll never forget hearing the story about my late great-grandmother who would feed the two of my uncles that were light-skinned and not their dark-skinned brothers. Once, one of my uncles got mad because he didn't like his other brothers to be left out, so he told her that if the rest of his brothers couldn't eat too, that he was not going to eat either. So instead of feeding all of them, she sent him back outside hungry with the rest of them. Now, I never met my great-grandmother, but I'm sure life wasn't too easy for her, especially not back then because she was raised back in the slave days. You would think she wouldn't have treated her own blood that way, but this racism within our own race has been going on for at least a century. We, as a people, and not just as the white race and the black race, but as one race under God, need to learn to love everybody, regardless of how they look. I have never heard of a white person treating another white person differently because his or her shade of white was a little more tanned. They are just white; there are no dark-skinned or light-skinned white people.

It's bad enough that racism still exists between blacks, whites, and every other race, but things are really starting to get out of hand and all of it is really uncalled for. I really wish that everyone would stop judging others by the color of their skin, but that's not the case and I don't think we will ever be rid of prejudiced people, but this is just something to think about. God made us all and everything around us and he didn't mean for everybody to look the same or be the same color, nor did he make any mistakes. So if we all realized that and stopped trying to determine if Jesus was white, black, or Indian, the world would be a better place. But in the meantime, just try to lift others up instead of putting them down.

Chapter 6

What Every Woman Must Do
to Find Her Soul Mate

It's simple; release all men from your past. You have to cleanse yourself of every man you have ever been intimate with, any man that you ever let in your heart, and most of all, your mind. You need to take a spiritual laxative. Your soul mate will treat you the way you deserve to be treated, but as long as you are carrying around that excess baggage from those other men or that other no good man, then you will never be able to fully receive YOUR man. In a deep conversation between women, a wise and insightful preacher brought to our attention something you would think most women already knew. But to sum it all up, she said, "How are you supposed give yourself to your man when you are carrying around all that weight of the other men from your past?" For some women, the men from their past are still in the present, holding them back from the salvation of having the "One." Give yourself a spiritual laxative and cleanse yourself of those past relationships, drama, and men with whom you have been exclusive with. You need to get some time by yourself, have a one on one with God, and confess it all to Him. Repent, and just let it go. And you have to leave it there. You can't let it go and turn around and go back to messing with the same man or men. You can't start the drama back up and you can't get sucked into the darkness by the rest of the players out there who are only after one thing. If you do, then you haven't let go and you can't move on to your man. Some of you may already have your man, but you just haven't released all those other men so you have all of them built up inside of you. You have to give up the ghost and do it now before the right one is gone. Have you ever wondered why your relationships don't work or why you can't find a good man for yourself? This could be the very problem. I thought I knew when I had reunited with my soul mate, but we were so out of sync before because I was carrying around baggage from my past and so was he. Therefore, he and I were unequally yoked and we couldn't work at that time.

If you've been hurt, all you need to do to move on is forgive the ones that hurt you and then you need to forgive yourself. If you have any last minute things to say, put them on paper. Write a letter or send it in an email. Some people are strong enough to talk face-to-face, but that never worked for me because one of two things will happen. He will either lay down his best sweet talking skills and before you know it, you'll be right back where you started, or it will turn into a huge argument with you two talking *at* each other rather than talking *to* each other. There will be yelling and both of you will end up saying harsh things to each other and it will only end up with you hating each other. It will cause you more unnecessary stress. If you send an email or write a letter, you can say everything that you need to say and then move on. He can't yell back at you, nor can you argue on paper. And make sure you've got it all down because you don't want to leave out anything that would cause you to have to call him back. You have to get that final closure.

Chapter 7

Never Make a Man your Priority When He Only Makes You an Option

There is way too much attention put into men. If we spent more of our time working on ourselves and less time worrying about these men, we would be better off and, most of all, stronger. There should be nothing painful about being in love. Love is supposed to be easy – not always smooth sailing, because every relationship has problems – but if you are crying every day or every other day because of ongoing drama, take it from me, it's not really love. Mary J. Blige has a song called "Ain't Really Love" that sums this up really well.

Why would you make a man your priority when men are going to be extinct in about twenty years anyway? But I'll get into that in another chapter. We have to stop using loneliness as an excuse to put up with anything when there are plenty of women who are managing just fine without a man – raising kids, working a fulltime job, and going to school. We are the strongest beings on earth, but we give these men so much power and influence over us that we don't realize how strong we really are. There's nothing wrong with giving yourself to a man, but make sure he's worth your time. If he does drugs, lives at home but isn't paying a single bill, and doesn't know how to pull his pants up, he still has a lot to learn and he's probably not the one for you right now. Give him a chance to get himself together, and in the mean time, keep it moving.

Chapter 8

Rising Above Insecurities

How many women remember this infamous line from the movie "Baby Boy" with Tyrese and Taraji Henson? When arguing about Jodi messing around with other women, Jodi asked Yvette, "Why you so insecure girl?" And this famous line that we, as women, use way too often? "Jodi, if I'm insecure, it's because you made me this way." You keep letting him do you wrong, and when you break up, it's only for a minute. Then, you're right back together. It's like you're trying to go nowhere. If you have broken up fifteen times in the past year, that's a problem. He doesn't have marriage anywhere on his mind, but you are thinking that one day, you're going to get a ring.

Stop crying to your man, asking that one question that every victim has used, "Why are you doing this to me?" Because he's only doing what you allow him to do to you, so technically, you are doing it to yourself. Thus, you are the victim. Get yourself out of that victim mentality. If you can't look your family and friends in the face because you are too ashamed of yourself for what you have been putting up with, then you don't need to be putting up with it. If you have to be making up excuses trying to justify the things that he has done wrong, then he is not the one – at least not right now.

He's going to have to go through some things first and find out what you are really worth. And it shouldn't take any man years and years to figure out if you are the one. Every married man that I have talked to said that he knew after only being friends with their wives for a few months that she was the one he was going to marry.

Women are precious to the Lord, and he would never want us to endure any kind of pain caused by a man. We give these men too much power and leave ourselves with little or no power at all. Then, when you threaten to leave, they try to make you feel guilty. They think they are so good at trying to convince us that we wouldn't find anybody like them. So your saying that I won't find a man who will disrespect me, cheat on me, and use and abuse me mentally and emotionally like you did? GOOD! That's the whole object of the game – to get somebody better than him. If you keep running into these guys who don't have real jobs, they still want to run the streets and keep their options open with other women while being with you. They have more drama than females do. If you keep attracting those types of so-called men, then you won't know the real deal when he comes. Your mind has been programmed to accept the bull crap and you don't know how to receive a good man when he comes.

Chapter 9

Women Make the World Go Round

Can you imagine the world without the female being? A lot of people refuse to believe this, but women make the world go round – not money. These men wouldn't know what to do with themselves without the existence of a woman. Ninety percent of them would commit suicide because they wouldn't be able to handle a world with no women. The rest of them are gay and it wouldn't matter to them anyway. But seriously, who would take care of these children running around? Who would be there to give them home cooked dinners, clean the houses, make sure appointments are kept, boost their egos, have sex with them, and keep them sane? That was just a little something for you to think about.

"When one door of happiness closes, another opens, but often we look so long at the closed door that we do not see the one that has been opened for us."

Helen Keller

Chapter 10

Beaten and Mistreated

Statistics show that two to four million women are battered by their spouse or intimate partner per year. You need to think about this before you complain about how hard you may have it, because there is someone out there whose situation is a lot worse than yours. Every 15 seconds, a woman is battered, and ladies, this is not good at all. There is nothing lovely about a man beating on you. Get out and get out now!!! Don't let any man put his hands on you. There is nowhere in the bible that says thou shall beat thy woman. And nowhere does physical abuse spell love. Take it from my friend who grew up watching her mother drink until she fell in a rut. She watched as her mom got beaten by men. Since her mother wasn't the perfect role model for her and her siblings, she depended on her grandmother to teach her the ways of the world. After her grandma passed away, she had to deal with the immaturities of her mom leaving for days at a time and she was left to make sure her brother and sister were fed. They would go without lights and heat just so their mom could run the streets, not knowing when or if she would come home. When she turned 13, she met this boy, and he was there for her, and at 17, she married him. How thankful she was to finally get away from that stressful situation that she had been in for years, putting up with her mom's mishaps and drinking. She had a man that loved her and cared about her well-being, her best friend. *Finally, someone who won't hurt me,* she thought. Now, being married at a young age, she didn't know much about taking care of everyday responsibilities like paying bills, establishing credit, and most of all, working. She settled into a lifestyle of cooking, cleaning, and fulfilling her husband's needs, or so she thought. Then, things started to change. Her husband became more and more distant; then came the cheating. She told me, "This is what happens when you give a man total control over your life. You give up your own life for his." He would take her out to eat and buy her all the fine things she could ever want. Then, he would drop her off at home so he could go be with his women. Waiting at home for him to return, she noticed a difference in his demeanor when he walked in the house nearly three hours later. Of course, she questioned him about being with another woman, and he snapped. The other woman had obviously pissed him off before he came home, and to him, who better to take it out on than his wife? He turned off all the lights so she couldn't see and beat her like she was nothing. Trying to fight back and screaming, "Why are you jumping on me? I haven't done anything to you!" She left that fight with a broken jaw and a bloodied and bruised face.

She recalled another incident when a cousin of hers stopped by to see her and the kids. Thinking that he was gone since his car wasn't in the yard and he'd told her he was leaving, she confided in her cousin by telling her that she was tired of all the fights and she was leaving him and she was getting another man, when out jumps this fool from the closet door.

"My mouth dropped," she said. Needless to say, that led to another beating.

"Oh, you think you bad now," he told her. Thinking he would teach her a lesson, he would leave her at home with the kids with no electricity, no food, no phone, nothing for days at a time. She didn't know the first thing about getting the electricity turned back on. It seemed hopeless when she decided that enough was enough and she was going to move on with her life. After she filed for a restraining order, she had found her a decent man whom she thought would protect her, but when that husband got wind of another man, he broke into the house in the middle of the night and she woke up to him standing over her with a gun. He walked over to the other side of the bed and tapped on the man with the gun. "That was a bad night," she explained, "but luckily nobody got killed."

She also remembered the time he came home when she was asleep and he jumped on her and beat her so badly she almost passed out. She said that somehow she managed to break away from him and ran to the front door. She said that she was butt naked and he was chasing her through the house when she finally got out the door and ran to a neighbor's house for help, pouring blood without so much as a bra and a pair of panties on.

After fighting for so long, she decided one day that she had enough and got another restraining order against him. Then, here he comes with pampers for the baby. "Leave them on the porch and I'll get them later," she said. She waited some time, thinking he was gone, and went to open the door, when suddenly, she felt a kick to the face and then he was in the house.

"You think a piece of paper is going to keep me from you?" Then, he pulled out a gun and stuck it in her mouth. She said he told her that he would kill her, go back there and kill their kids, and then kill himself because there would be nothing else to live for. Then, he began taking off her clothes. She begged him to stop, but he didn't. With the children in the house, he raped her while still having the gun pointed down her throat. It had gotten so bad that she was fighting every week. If she wasn't fighting back at him, she was fighting the different women that he had cheated with. She said that some days, he would threaten to kill her and she would stab him out of self-defense.

The most memorable and most shocking incident happened when she questioned him about being high on marijuana. She called him on everything that he had been doing wrong, when finally, she struck the right nerve. The argument had led to the porch where her niece was standing by her side. As the argument escalated, he pulled out his gun again and pointed it at her head. But this time, she had enough of backing down from him, so she kept fussing. She yelled and yelled at him, saying that he didn't have the balls to pull the trigger, that he wasn't a real man, and on and on and on, when suddenly, she remembered a cold chill came over her and she pushed her niece out of the way when, POW. He shot her. From there, all she could remember was thinking, *This is it; I'm going to die today.* As her sister ran to her rescue, she was able to mumble to her not to let anyone take her kids. Then it was lights out. She had been shot on the side of her neck and if she hadn't moved her head to push her niece back, the bullet would have gone through her temple, killing her instantly. After her recovery, she went before the judge and begged for the case to be dropped. She actually stood up for him in court where she didn't press the first charge. Thinking that a near-death experience such as that would be her breaking point, it wasn't. After recovering at the hospital, she was released to go home. She was so lost that she fell into a terrible state of depression. She lay on the couch in the living room day after day, week after week. By this time, their daughter had noticed that her dad would pick up some other kids at the daycare that was across the street from their house. Then, one day, her daughter asked, "Mommy, why is daddy always over there picking up those other kids?" After hearing those words come from her daughter, she snapped. She went in the kitchen, grabbed a knife, and headed across the street with all intentions of killing him. She tried to go after him when one of the ladies that worked there grabbed her and told her that he wasn't worth it and that if she didn't calm down, she would have to call the police and they would send her to jail. By this time, he had jumped in the car with the kids and driven off. She went back home, still depressed, and decided that she didn't want to go on living. She went to the nearest gas station, got one dollar's worth of gasoline, and went back home. She had planned to set the house on fire and kill herself and her two daughters when one of her daughters said, "Mommy, are you going to kill us?" And it was those words that snapped her back into place and she never thought about killing herself or her kids again.

The breaking point finally came one night after he had sworn off the other women and all the wrongdoings. Everything seemed to have finally started to work itself out, but that female intuition, that conscience that we women have, kicked into gear – but this time, it was in overdrive. So she got in the car and started driving, looking for him to find what woman it was this time. That gut feeling led her straight to him at another woman's house. There was his car in the driveway, as she suspected. Yelling from outside, here he comes out of the house, zipping his pants up. *Somebody is going to die tonight,* was all she kept telling herself. The more he tried to push her back in the car, the more pissed she became, until she snapped again. She shoved him, went to the trunk, pulled out an iron wrench, and before she knew anything, she had struck him in the back of the head. He went down like Apollo Creed did in *Rocky* when he fought that Russian. Fragments of his head and blood began gushing out and she said to herself, *Well, he's dead.* By this time, the other woman was screaming and calling the police. She tried to pull his body in the house while trying to avoid letting his wife get close to her. But it wasn't over. She wanted to make that chick suffer for cheating with her husband. The woman managed to close the door quickly before she could get to it. Yelling and kicking in the door, she was not going to stop until she got her hands on that chick. BAM, BAM, BAM! She was trying to break the hinges off the door, when all of a sudden, she was rushed by the police. They locked her up and threw all kind of charges at her. They set the bond so high that no one could get her out. Needless to say, he was rushed to the hospital where he later recovered from what could have been the end of him. She said the longer she sat in jail, the more she realized that it was finally time for her to let go. She had snapped and almost taken his life after trying to stand up for him in court when he shot and almost killed her. That was enough. That was the final breaking point. It was over and there was no turning back. Prior to that incident, she had started making an exit plan of how she was going to get out of the marriage, get her kids, and escape to a place where he couldn't harm her again, and that's just what she did.

The awesome thing about this story is that if you met her right now, you wouldn't be able to tell that she had been abused the way she was. She has met the most wonderful man who appreciates her, brings her breakfast in bed, goes to church with her, and loves her kids as if they were his own. And last but certainly not least, he doesn't beat her. She is proud to say that through prayer, her family, and her close friends, she was able to forgive her ex-husband and finally move on with her life. "I thank God every day that He helped me get through that situation," she says.

The thing that I admire about her the most is that she didn't let the wrongdoings of her ex-husband cause her to become bitter and hateful. She has unmovable faith and a very encouraging personality. Before, she didn't know what it meant to have her own money, nor did she know how to take care of herself because everything was under his control. But now, she has been blessed with a good job, she bought her own car, and she has her own place. Many women in this situation think that there is little or no hope, but she is a living testimony that you can get out of an abusive relationship alive. "The most important tool is to have an exit plan," she explained. Get someone you can confide in and have them help you and your kids get out. If you don't have anyone that you can trust, you need to call 1-800-799-SAFE (7233). You are worth it, no matter what he says. You are worth it and you deserve better. Get out and get out now, before it's too late. Do it for your kids, and if you don't have kids, then do it for yourself. Here are some signs that you need to look out for. One of the first signs indicating that you may be headed towards this situation is if he moves you away from your family. You aren't allowed to hang out with your friends. You really can't leave the house without him being with you. Some of you that have jobs are allowed to go to work and maybe the grocery store. Then, it's home to fix his meals, make his plate the way he wants it, iron his clothes, give up the TV to him, and give him sexual pleasure whenever he wants it. Then you are not allowed to do anything or go anywhere without his say so. The next thing you know, he has complete control over what used to be your life. Now, there is nothing wrong with catering to your man, as long as it doesn't turn into slaving for your man, and there is a big difference. Pay attention to the warning signs and leave before it gets physical because there are lots of women who were not as fortunate to get out alive.

Chapter 11

Recovery after Being Raped

Here's another scenario of your everyday woman who went through a storm and is now sitting on top of the world. Someone very near and dear to me was raped by someone that we both knew. According to Battered Women, Domestic Violence, and Rape reports, one third of all women have been raped in their lifetime and 80% of all rapists know their victims.

This particular incident took place at a party where there was a lot of heavy drinking and smoking. The boy, who was obviously high and drunk, followed her as she tried to go to the bathroom and managed to corner her in where she couldn't get out. She tried to scream for help, but the music in the apartment was too loud for anyone to hear her. She said he started trying to rub and kiss on her and she kept trying to push him off. When she did manage to get out of the bathroom, he came right behind her and threw her on the bed. She tried everything she could to get him off her, but he was a big athlete and overpowered her. She could do nothing but cry. He pulled her clothes off and raped her. She said after he was finished, he must have realized what he had done, and quickly became remorseful, which doesn't excuse his actions at all. She said she felt so nasty and violated and remembers being in the shower for over an hour trying to wash away what had just happened. She was too afraid and embarrassed to report him.

I was overseas when that incident took place, and when I found out about it, I was outraged. I wanted to have him hanged for doing that to her. I was always like the mother figure for my friends, and when I was around, I didn't let anything happen to them. For a long time, I felt bad because I wasn't there to save her. I knew that if I had been there, it would never have taken place. I wish that there were something I could have done to make it better, but the truth is that it was his fault, not mine or hers. He is the dog that took advantage of her. He did not deserve to walk the streets, let alone come in contact with any woman after what he had done, but I told her that even though he didn't go to jail for it, he would not have a good life until he repented for his sin. For a long time, she thought it was her fault, and sometimes, that's the way people make it seem. When someone is raped, you can't point the blame at anybody but the rapist. I'll never forget the day I was almost raped by someone I knew and had known for a while. It was a friendly visit that turned sour. I never did anything to lead him on. I didn't have on any revealing clothing, but that didn't matter to him. The minute I noticed a change in his tone and face, I didn't feel comfortable, so I tried to leave, but he grabbed me, pushed me down on the sofa, and climbed on top of me. I yelled for him to get off and pushed him as hard as I could but that wasn't enough. When he tried to pull my shorts off, I kneed him in his stomach, and when he fell on me, I pushed him on the floor, quickly jumped up, and ran out the door. I hopped in my car as fast as I could and sped off with my heart about to jump out of my chest. I didn't call the police, nor did I tell my parents. I just figured that since he didn't actually commit the act, I shouldn't say anything, and that is a big mistake that a lot of females make when they are faced with this type of situation. But you should definitely tell somebody because you could save another person from enduring the same thing. As for that guy, he ended up getting into trouble for his wild actions. I said this to my friend and I'll say it to any woman who has been raped, "You are the victim and there is no way that you should let anybody make you feel bad about a man raping you." Outside of murder, that is one of the most disgusting and brutal things a man can do to a female and I don't feel like the laws are harsh enough on these types of predators. I always tell people that you cannot treat people any way you like and expect to get away with it. Karma is real and it's no fun when you are on the reaping end; what goes around will come back to you. It's been a few years since I saw the guy who raped my friend, and it was when I went back down to Charleston for another friend's graduation. I was eight months pregnant when I saw him, and I remember my heart stopping like I had seen a ghost. I felt this cold feeling come over me that almost put me in labor and it was a good thing I was pregnant because had I not been, there is no telling what I would have done to that sorry excuse for a man. I couldn't speak or say anything to him. When the graduation class came out of the building, I got myself together enough to congratulate them, speak to the family, and leave. And I haven't seen him since.

We know of other women who have been through

this type of situation and didn't have the help and support to get over what happened. It traumatized them and led them to become very promiscuous with different men. If you are one of these women, I beg you to seek counseling from someone. Talk to your pastor or someone you can trust to help put your mind at ease because you don't want one man's taking advantage of you to be a reason for you letting several men do the same thing to you at your own will. You have to think about your health and well-being and it's not safe out there at all. It's been years since that incident took place, and as far as my friend goes, I am very happy to report that after lots of prayer and support from her family and her real friends, she was able to get over that horrible situation, is now happily married to the love of her life, and is well on her way to owning her first beauty salon.

Chapter 12

A Woman's Worth

If I could count the years spent by women waiting on men to change and get married to them, I am sure the numbers would be outrageous. One of my friends who is married now once told me that he knew when he met his wife that she would be the one he married. They were friends first, he mentioned, and after some time passed, he knew what he had to do. There was no uncertainty. One thing that stuck out the most to me was when he said that it's okay for your man to be uncertain about some things, but the one thing that you don't want from your man is him being uncertain about whether he wants to be with you, because a man knows when he has found that special lady. There are no doubts, ifs, ands, or buts about it. He knows that you are the one. If he is back and forth from month to month, and in some cases, year after year, and he still hasn't decided if you are the "One," leave him be. How much more of your life are you going to waste waiting on him to make up his mind about what he wants to do and who he wants to be with. I've been there and done that and you can never get that lost time back. Ladies, know your worth and own it.

Chapter 13

You and Your Kids Can
Have the World

Ladies, we are wonderful creatures, and when you are blessed with the ability to have children, you become invincible. There is no greater feeling than looking at the little person that you have carried for all those months, that you have felt kick you, and that has caused you to put on some extra unwanted pounds. I used to be a lover and a fighter, and I still am to a certain extent, but having kids has slowed me down a lot. Yes, it gets hard, but you should always remember that the Lord never puts any more on you than you can bear.

When it comes to raising kids, we need to get back into that old school upbringing. I remember when my parents had company, I was always sent to my room because my momma said that kids had no business in the room when grown folks were talking. Nowadays, we let our kids hear and see everything, and that's not good. As a mother, you can't let your daughters see mommy with a different man every few weeks because if she doesn't grow up not wanting to be anything like you, she will grow up thinking it's okay to run through different men just like you. As mothers, you can't let your sons see you stay with men that beat and disrespect you, because they may grow up thinking it's okay to hit on women, thus teaching them to become another statistic. We, as parents, also need to instill in our sons that sleeping with a bunch of women does not make you a man because the last thing the world needs is another playboy running around, not thinking about the consequences of sleeping with anybody and everybody.

I have two beautiful little girls for whom I would climb the highest mountain if I thought it would keep them from the many hurts, harms, and dangers of this world. As parents, we have to be very careful of what we expose our children to. You need to speak positively to your kids every day, and teach them that they can do anything they want, as long as they go about it in the right way. My parents always raised me not to be jealous or envious of anybody, but to make things happen for myself. And that created the go-getter that's still inside me today. When I was growing up, if there was something I really wanted, I went for it. Why waste time being envious of someone else when you can have it too as long as you go about it in the right way? My babies are too young to understand that now, but as soon as they reach that age, I will be instilling a lot of those same qualities in them that my parents instilled in me.

First of all, every mother knows that it's no easy task raising children and no one's running around handing out medals or giving up some extra cash for you doing a good job. But at the end of the day, God makes no mistakes and our children are here for a reason – all children are. We, as mothers, do what we have to do for our children – not what we want – at least, not the real mothers. We know what it means to make sacrifice after sacrifice for our kids. Sometimes that requires putting your life on hold in order for your kids to have the love and support they need. I take my hat off to women who have full-time jobs, go to school, and take care of their kids. It was 2003 when I was pulled out of school to go overseas, and in 2005, I got pregnant with my first daughter. I was able to attend classes while I was pregnant, but after I gave birth and was still working, it almost seemed impossible for me to come up with a schedule that would fit me going to work, going to school, and taking care of my baby without inconveniencing someone else. One day, I decided that I was going back to school no matter what it took. I prayed long and hard for the Lord to make a way for me to get the ball rolling and go back to school. The life I was living just wasn't for me anymore and I knew that getting back in school was just the boost I needed to help me get on the right track to making a significant change in my life and my career. I am now enrolled in school, still working full-time as a single mother of two taking care of business, and you can do it too. If you are a single parent, don't keep yourself down just because it didn't work out with you and your child's father. See, it's easy for men to help you make the babies, but after you have them, the man's life really doesn't have to change that much. He still gets to do what he wants while you do what you have to do. At the end of the day, it's your life that gets altered, not theirs. Nothing compares to the things a mother does for her child.

Another mistake I see a lot of mothers make when they have children out of wedlock is listening to the wrong people. Rule number one: don't let anybody make you feel ashamed just because you have kids and may not be married. You just turn your life over to God and let Him use you and He'll send you your husband. Don't be so concerned with these so-called Christians that judge and look down on everybody like they have never sinned. You just work on bettering yourself and establishing a solid foundation so that your children won't want to make the same mistakes that you have.

One reason some people won't pick up a book or go to church is because they really don't want to hear right from wrong, even though they already know what they should be doing. It's called denial because they know that once you receive it, you will be held accountable for it. I've said it before and I'll say it again, God doesn't make mistakes, and every baby that is born is born for a reason. It may not have happened under the circumstances that you wanted, but that child has a purpose.

The last concern I have regarding our children is the fact that nowadays, there is something about sex everywhere you turn, and it's getting to our children at a young age. We have to start talking to our children about sex at an early age because it's nothing like how it used to be. You can't just tell your son to make sure he wears a condom because he can bring home more than just a baby. You can't just tell your daughter to make sure she doesn't bring home any babies because there's more stuff out there now that you can catch. The HIV and STD rates among young people are alarming, and that's not including the number of teens that don't even know they are infected with a disease. If there was ever a time to teach abstinence to our children, it would be now. Of course, we live in the real world and we can't be around our children 24/7, but we still need to have that talk with them. These kids are doing more than just kissing at these parties. They have these parties in high school now called Rainbow Parties, and what happens is a group of boys get together, come up with a location, and invite a few girls to show up. Each girl has a different shade of lipstick that she wears and the boys compete with each other to see who has the most shades of lipstick on his penis at the end of the party. So that tells you what these girls are stooping to and these young men don't realize what they are getting into and that's how STDs get passed around. I've heard young girls say that they perform oral sex because they can't get pregnant. We have to wake up, mothers and fathers, and really start paying some attention to our children before it's too late. We have to teach them that they can grow up to be anything they want if they follow the right path.

The Beam in Our Eyes.
Why do you notice the splinter in your brother's eye, but do not perceive the wooden beam in your own? Luke 6:41
A FEW YEARS BACK, I heard stories of people moving out of pews in Catholic churches to avoid sitting next to a man or woman who was divorced. I never saw this happen, and I certainly hope it was rare when it did. Nowadays divorce is unfortunately so commonplace that, if this kind of behavior were the norm, Sunday liturgies would see people in constant motion in search of a pew untouched be people from failed marriages.
This gospel passage is not about the pain of divorce. It's about hypocrisy and judging others. It's about having acute awareness of other people's failings, while ignoring our own. Although we may not be among the seat-changers, we need to think about that beam in our eye and forget about the splinters we see elsewhere. And remember, every pew is filled with sinners.
Prayer: Dear Jesus, help me see my faults and find the compassion needed to love my neighbor as you love us.

Paul Pennick

Chapter 14

Dating a Man Who Has a Child by another Woman

I'm selfish when it comes to my man, as every woman should be. You're not supposed to share your man with other women. Now, there is a difference between being selfish about your man and being insecure about your man. You know those women who can't let their man out of their sight without following him or trying to tag along because she's afraid of what might happen, especially women who are in relationships with men who have children with other women. Ladies, if you are in a relationship with a man who has kids with another woman, you need to realize that you can't come between that man and his child or his child's mother, nor should you want to. That was something that happened before you came into the picture, and there's nothing you can do about it. If you are not secure enough to deal with a man having a child with someone else, then you need to look for someone who doesn't have kids, because if he's a real man, that child will always be a part of his life, and you have to realize that the mother will be too. I do owe a great deal of gratitude and respect to all the men out there who stand up and still take care of their kids even though they may not be with the child's mother.

Chapter 15

Young and Naïve

I was 19 years old when I first met the ultimate bachelor, and he was 26. This story is a typical case of a naïve girl getting played by an older man. Here it was, 2002, and I was in Charleston going to college. I was introduced to this guy through a mutual friend. She told me how much he had his stuff together, but little did I know that there was an ex-girlfriend out there who was 4 pennies short of a nickel. Now, when my friend finally told me about the ex, it was too late. All hell had already broken loose. She called me in her room to tell me that a girl she used to hang with was on the phone and wanted to talk to me.

"Who is she and what does she want with me?"

"Oh, it's his ex."

So I get on the phone. "Who are you and how do you know me?"

She told me that she was his girlfriend and she wanted to know what kind of relationship I had with him.

"Excuse me, you must be mistaken because I'm his girlfriend and you are just an ex that he no longer deals with."

"Oh really?" she said. "Well I'm going to prove it.

I'm calling him on three-way and I want you to just listen."

She calls and he answers on the second ring, "What's up?"

"Hey baby, I thought you were coming over here?"

"I am; I just got finished playing basketball with the boys. Did you get that money for me?"

"Yea boo, I'll have it for you when you get here, okay? And by the way, Olivia is on the phone. I guess this is your girlfriend too, huh?"

Click. He hung up.

Now I'm ready to fight. I called his phone about ten times and of course, he didn't answer. I guess he was trying to figure out how he was going to get out of this one. About four hours went by and then my phone rang. By this time, I had taken his name out of my phone and hoped that I would forget the number.

"What?" I said.

"Look, it's not what you think. That girl's crazy. I'm not messing with her. We're just friends and she's loaning me some money. I told her that I was seeing somebody else and she's going crazy about it. She used to be my girlfriend and when I broke up with her she tried to commit suicide; that's the only reason I keep in touch with her, so she won't completely lose her mind."

He then told me to ask my friend about her. So I called my girl and asked her if the girl tried to kill herself. "Yeah girl, she's crazy."

She slit her wrist when he tried to breakup with her. Well, that worked for me, so now I'm mad at the ex. Here's a good rule of thumb, ladies. Never go after the chick because she is a victim too and the sad thing is she doesn't know it. Deal with the man because nothing ever happens that he doesn't let happen, so stop trying to fight that other girl, even if she knows about you, because it only goes as far as he lets it go. I'll say it again. These women out here don't care about you. First of all, they don't have any respect for themselves so you already know that they don't care for you. You should expect that kind of behavior from the other women. He should be the one to put an end to any disrespect brought on by another woman anyway. If he doesn't nip that mess in the bud, let him go. It's not worth it.

Some time went by and I didn't hear much from the ex. I still had this feeling in the pit of my stomach every time I went over there, but I let him convince me that it was nothing. I was giving this man money and I did a lot for him. And the thing is, with some, they will use you as long as you let them or until they have used you up and there is nothing left. You would think I would have known something when every time we went out to eat, he never paid, not once. He wouldn't even pay at a place like Burger King. We got in there – and this was back when they had the buy two whoppers, two fries, and two drinks for like 5.49 – and he didn't want that. His sorry behind wanted to get the most expensive sandwich on the menu, as if he was paying. I'll never forget the time I had received my back pay from the military that was over 900 dollars. All of a sudden, his car was in the shop and it was going to cost him 300 to get it worked on. Do you know I went and cashed my little check and gave this man with a fulltime job 300 dollars to get his car fixed! It's been

7 years since that happened, and I still shake my head at myself for that one, thinking I was in love. I wasn't listening to anybody or that little voice inside my head that told me, "He's not the one, move on, he's just using you." I was sure it was love. Yeah, that's one-sided love that a lot of women find themselves caught up in. You constantly have to make excuses for his wrongdoings or try to prove his love for you to other people, when if he truly loved you, everyone would automatically see it. It was always "me, me, me" doing everything, and I can't remember him doing anything for me – not a birthday gift, a Valentine's Day card, Christmas gift, nothing. He told me once that we were going to Savannah for the weekend to get away. I had my bags packed and was ready to go. I pulled up at his apartment and out he comes with no bags and one of his boys talking about us driving my car to Savannah.

Now, I drove a mustang and everybody knows that it's a sports car that has extremely small back seats. His friend was about 6'2 and he was looking at me like I'm about to get in the backseat of my own car. I argued him up and down about how we already had a previous agreement that we were taking his car because I didn't want to put a lot of miles on my car. Here it is, twenty minutes later, and we are finally on the road on our way to Savannah with his friend in the backseat of my car. His phone rings, and at first, he ignores it. Then, I told him, "Hey, your phone is ringing."

He answered it and said, "What's up? I told you I was going to Savannah."

Now his friend in the back is trying to distract me by talking about what kind of tattoo he wanted to get and it worked. We got to Savannah and I didn't think anything else of the phone call because I was still pissed off about us being in my car and him bringing his friend on the trip that was supposed to just be for us. So, needless to say, we didn't spend the night. We ended up going for him to get a tattoo and to walk around the mall with him walking either ten feet in front of me or ten feet behind me. By the time we got back to Charleston, I was steaming hot because he had my car going 95 to 100 on the freeway with that idiot in the back telling him to go faster. I let my anger go for about five seconds when we dropped his friend off at home and he went to get out of the car and couldn't hardly stand up straight because he had been cramped up in my backseat for over an hour. Now, you'd think that was it for me, but nope; I got over that and stayed with him.

A few weeks went by and I was getting ready to head to his apartment. He had always told me to call him before I left campus, so I called him and a girl answered the phone. I asked her who she was and where he was.

"Oh, he's in the shower. Is this Olivia?"

"Yes it is. Do I know you?"

"No, you don't, but I'll tell him you called," and she hung up.

Oh, hell no! I called his phone back and nobody answered. By this time, I was in my car, on the way over there, pissed off again and hoping I could catch him so it would be over for real this time. I got there and beat on the door. He comes to the door with this smile on his face, trying to hug me.

"Oh no, where's your little girlfriend?"

"What are you talking about?" he said, telling me that it was his roommate's girlfriend and he was letting her use his phone while he was in the shower. Can you believe I actually fell for that, and shortly after, we left to go out to eat, of course, driving my car? And as always, he didn't pay.

Now here's when you know you need to stop and get out. I went back home for the weekend and my roommate and our mutual friend went bowling with him and some buddies he introduced them to. This crazy ex of his sees him out with my girls and blows up on him. No sooner do I get back, I hear about it from my roommate – not him. So I'm ready to go over there to see what he has to say about this, and he tells me before I could leave campus not to drive my car over there. So I tell my roommate what's going on and ask her for her truck. Now, my roommate was the feisty type, so she decides to wait a few minutes and then follow me over there in my car just in case something popped off. I said that was cool, not thinking anything of it. When I got there, there was no sign of the ex. I went upstairs, he and I talked about it, and he explained that she saw my car over there a few times and said if she saw my car over there again, she was going to mess up his car and mine. Now, at this point, I'm like, *I should have driven my car because I wish that chick would have tried to mess with my pony.*

He tells me again that she's crazy and that he doesn't want to provoke her. So we put a movie in and tried to relax. Now, he and I, we were supposed to be there by ourselves, or so we thought. But next thing I know, his bedroom door flies open. The only light that's on is coming from his TV, so I can't see who is standing in the door, but I can tell that the person is short, so I immediately rule out his roommate. Then, she flips the light on, and it's who I assume to be his ex, because until now, I'd never seen the chick before.

Then, he says, "What? You stole my key?"

I looked at him as I was standing up and said, "How the hell can she steal your key?"

"Oh, I was over here earlier today. He didn't tell you?"

Then, she saw my toothbrush by the bed and asked him if he was letting me spend the night. At this point, I was ready to football tackle him across the room, but I remembered that a friend of mine had warned me that the girls there carried knives and blades, so please believe, I was ready. I had my knife in my pocket and I quickly stuck my hand in there just in case she made any false moves. He walked her in the living room and they started arguing.

I hurried up, called my roommate, and told her that the ex was there, when all of a sudden, I heard two female voices in the living room. Little did I know, my roommate was around the corner and she said, "Girl, I'll be up there in two minutes, it's on!"

I walked out of the room and I saw another girl trying to pull the ex away from him and she was yelling, "He's not worth it! Let him have her! Let's go!"

By the time I could say anything, my roommate had busted in the door. "What? Y'all think y'all gonna jump on my roommate?" She came and grabbed my knife and it was on from there.

Now, he was standing there and hadn't said a word. So I said, "Tell her, Jamal. Tell her that I'm the one you are with and that she needs to move on with her life."

But he said nothing.

She looked at me and said, "You're so stupid. You think he hadn't been with me? Do you remember the day when y'all were going to Savannah and his phone rang? That was me. And do you remember the night you called his phone and a female answered? That was me. Do you remember the time you came over here and he didn't come to the door? It's because he was in here with me. Yeah, I know all about your little red mustang, 'cause you remember that time he had your car for the weekend? He came by my job to bring me lunch."

Hearing those words was like taking three bullets to the chest. I was shell-shocked and I couldn't move. Then, he wasn't the only one on mute because I couldn't speak either. I just looked at him for a minute. Then, my voice came back and I told my roommate to give me my knife back. Now, this girl and I were standing a few feet apart from each other and I was ready to jump on her something serious when it dawned on me that although she was a problem, it was he that allowed her to be a bigger problem. By this time, her friend had convinced her that they needed to leave and she pulled her out the door. I went back to the room to get the rest of my stuff and then I was leaving. Before my roommate and I could make it to the end of the hallway, she had run back in the apartment to the kitchen, grabbed a butcher knife, and was headed out the door towards me. He grabbed her by her arm and took the knife out her hand. By this time, my roommate was trying to pull me out of the apartment and her friend was trying to pull her. The next thing I knew, there were police sirens downstairs and she and the friend took off. Needless to say, the police ended up coming, and by that time, she and her friend had sped off and I was sitting at the bottom of the stairs when they ran up to me, asking where he was. I pointed up and they went to his door and beat until he finally answered. By this time, my roommate was trying to get me to leave, but my mind was somewhere else. I couldn't move. Then, the officer came back downstairs and told me that they had talked to him and he told them that neither one of us was his girlfriend and that he wanted us to leave him alone and not come back to his apartment again. Those words snapped me back into place. I looked at my roommate, unable to hold back my tears, and we left. After putting up with all of that, I was too mentally exhausted to even think about taking him back. I had a lot going for myself and there were a lot of nice guys that were asking me out, but I never gave them the time or day because I was so stuck on stupid. I started spending more time with my teammates, I made some new friends through a pageant I was in, and after some time, I was over him. After I had moved on, he started calling me back, talking about how he was ready to settle down and get married, but little did he know, his time had expired. I was so much happier without him than when I was with him, and after getting a glimpse of that, I wouldn't have dared to go back to all that unnecessary drama. There was one time that I got weak and almost went back to him, but one of my dear friends told me that I would be setting myself up for failure, and to prove it, he drove me by my ex's apartment early that morning. Guess whose car was in the parking lot? That was all I needed to see and I haven't been back since. What I learned from that bad relationship is that a man will tell you and another woman everything you want to hear and he will do what is necessary to please both of you so he can have his cake and eat it too. He will tell her one thing about you so she doesn't think you are a threat and then tell you stuff about her to make you think she isn't a threat. It's all a part of the game they play. The funny thing is, a few years later, after I left that school, I got a phone call from him, and things weren't going too well for him. He had been through hell and back and he just wanted to see how I was doing. His karma came back at him hard, and even though he didn't apologize for his actions, I knew he was feeling the backlash, and I haven't heard from him since.

Chapter 16

"APB for Promise Keepers"

Promise Keepers, where are you? It's time for you to blow up again. The world is screaming for powerful, good, stable, Christian men who know what they want out of life and are answering to what God has called them to do. If you don't know what Promise Keepers are, you need to do some research. They are Christian men who have rallies and gatherings to teach about the word of God and how men need to be held accountable. They really define the purpose God had planned for men and how you need to live up to that promise by being men of God. They are about being good husbands, fathers, leaders, and providers. We need more young men to get on board and start changing this world before it's too far gone.

The divine order is supposed to go God, man, woman, child, but somewhere down the line, the signals got crossed, and now man falls somewhere at the bottom and the woman had to step up and take on both roles. There are some good women out there who want nothing more than a good man of God, an unselfish man who really understands his role as a true man of God, and that's what the Promise Keepers represent. These men are not afraid of monogamy and they know how to treat women. I recommend the book *Seven Promises of a Promise Keeper* written by Bill Bright, Edwin Cole, Dr. James Dobson, Tony Evans, Bill McCartney, Luis Palau, Randy Phillips, and Gary Smalley. In this book, you will get the true definition of a Promise Keeper. It's time to wake up, men.

Chapter 17

Why Men Are Headed
Towards Extinction

Men, after you reach a certain age, it's no longer okay to use the manner in which you were brought up as an excuse for treating women wrong and living your life the way you do. You have to accept the fact that you are a grown man now and you are held responsible for your actions. You not having a father figure growing up can't be your crutch for the rest of your life. Stop using excuses for your doing wrong. Man up and take responsibility. Just like with the women, don't let the way you were brought up determine how you are going to live the rest of your life. You need to empower yourselves too, and start soon, before you become extinct. I really hate to say this, but at the rate a lot of men are going, you are headed towards extinction. Now, this is just my own opinion, so my predictions should not be taken personally, but I think men, or black men, at least, will be out of here soon unless some drastic changes take place. Every reason I have ends up with them being extinct. Think about this. According to the Bureau of Justice Statistics in 2008, 2,310,984 prisoners were held in federal of state prisons or in local jails. At midyear 2008, there were 4,777 black male inmates per 100,000 black males held in state and federal prisons and local jails as opposed to only 727 white male inmates per 100,000 white males. Male suicide rates are disturbing as well. Suicide is the eighth leading cause of death for all U.S. men according to National Center for Injury Prevention and Control. According to the U.S. Suicide Statistics, one year, there was a reported 25,907 male suicides with a 4 to 1 ratio of male suicides over female suicides. We really have to evaluate the facts. I'm not trying to doom men, but it's a sad reality that we need to take seriously. Look at the number of men who are homosexual and passing around AIDS and HIV. Look at the men killing men on the streets. All of these things are sending our men straight down, but maybe with the help of the Promise Keepers, preachers, leaders, and strong women, we can make a change. You can't tell me that anything isn't possible if you only had a little faith and determination. Prime example – we have Barack Obama for our president. That is enough in itself to want to change for the better.

Chapter 18

White Men Versus Black Men

I hate to play the race card, but we would be fooling ourselves if we thought that there were no differences between the two. White men and black men handle relationships completely differently. Don't believe me. Talk to some of our Caucasian brothers and sisters and they'll tell you how it works. Or just look at the statistics. More white men get married than black men by a long shot. First of all, white men aren't about shacking up with a woman for years and years at a time and popping out a couple of kids without even considering getting married. Oh no, after dating for some months, they know if you are the one or not, and if you are, there is the engagement that doesn't last for three years. A black man, on the other hand, is a completely different story. A black man will live with you, let you cook for him, be there for him, and take care of the kids, and next thing you know, it's been five years. You are still waiting on him to just wake up one day and say, "Baby, let's get married." Why would he do that when you already fulfill the duties of a wife without the actual marital commitment? So what is it about the word 'marriage' that scares most black men to death? What is so wrong with monogamy that drives some men away like you just asked them to get a catheter stuck up their butt? Men, you might want to start considering being with one woman because the HIV/AIDS cases are alarming, and if the thought of that doesn't scare you, how about these statistics? Did you know that 1.1 million persons are living with HIV in the U.S. according to the Centers for Disease Control and Prevention? And they are expecting that number to increase. And it's inevitable given the lifestyles that many Americans are choosing to live. But I have the answer, ladies. We have to step outside of our boxes. There's nothing wrong with dating a man outside our race, because from the looks of it, they are the ones that are getting married.

Chapter 19

Can a Cheating Man Change?

Why don't people believe in karma? By now, you would think that everybody knows that what goes around comes around. I guess not everybody, because there are so many men and women who are out there cheating and don't realize the repercussions of their actions – not yet, at least.

I'll use my friend as an example. He was the good guy, married with children, a true workaholic. But let me tell you how he lost everything. He strayed away from his marriage to another woman, and finally, his conscience ate him up so bad, he had to tell his wife. Even though she was devastated by the news, she chose to stay and try to work things out. I remember telling him that he needed to cut all communication with the other woman and never see her again. I said, "You were lucky; your wife stayed with you. But if she finds out that you are still in contact with this woman, it's going to be a bad day for you."

He was spending more time and money at his mistress' house than he was at his own. That other woman had his nose so up in the air that he didn't hear a word I said, and just as I suspected, his wife found out, and just like that, she was gone. When I tell you he went through hell and back, he really had reached rock bottom, and life as he knew it just wasn't the same anymore. He lost a lot of his clientele, lost his house, fell into bad health, missed out on quality time with his kids, and lost the love of his life. He only wished he could have gotten his life back with his wife and kids. Needless to say, that other woman has moved on with her life with another man. As you can see, the affair was so short-lived, and he is paying for it to this day.

So yes, this cheating man did change, but it was too late, because this time, she couldn't take him back. Which raises another question… Do all men cheat? That is one of the biggest mysteries to women. My theory is no, not all men cheat, but there are a large number of men who do and these loose women out here don't make it any easier on the men who are trying not to cheat. Because they will keep after him, throw it at him, throw it on him, show it to him, let him smell it, whatever it takes.

Now, a lot of the men who I have talked to about this have said that after it was over, they realized that the cheating really wasn't worth all the drama that came with it in the end. They also said that it depends on what you consider cheating. I asked one of my male classmates if he would cheat if he had a good woman, and his exact words were, "No, I wouldn't jeopardize what I got at home for another woman no matter how fine she is and it is not that good when you do it." I then asked him if he thought texting another woman was cheating, and he said that as far as texting goes, if you are entertaining someone else's thoughts and feelings while you are in a relationship, that's cheating. There are plenty of men that will risk letting a good woman go because they still want to provide a public service to every woman that is willing and able to be serviced. Men, at the end of the day, while you are running around on your women, looking for the next best thing, or just plain playing the field when you have a good woman, you might want to think about what she's worth. And to those of you with children who are cheating, when she finds out and moves on, it'll be a sad day for you when you see your child being raised by another man.

I'm always telling my male friends that if you have a good woman, you need to hold on to her because these other women of the world don't mean you any good. Everybody who is close to me has heard me say this. If you were in a bad car accident and your face got rearranged, who do you think would be there to take care of you? It wouldn't be that other woman who is always in the streets, bouncing from man to man and opportunity to opportunity. It would be that one true woman who has always been loyal to you. You know she's a good woman, but you let those outside influences steer you the wrong way. And men, by the time you realize what your woman is really worth to you, she could be gone. Don't be a Samson and let these Delilah's of the world convince you to turn your back on what is real, because you won't be able to handle it when it finally catches up to you.

Men, I know you have all heard the saying "you can't judge a book by its cover" and it may sound redundant, but it is true. I know you are very visual beings who get turned on instantly just by the way a woman looks. But you had better look a little deeper because everything that looks good isn't good for you.

A quick note to the women though – if your man really wants to cheat, he will. You can't be there all the time. It's never good to smother him; he'll just rebel. Just tell him what I tell men when it comes to cheating, "Break up with me first and I'll do the same for you." That's the most honest thing you can do for a woman. Even if she doesn't want to hear it, give her the respect of letting her go before you break her heart. Married men, sorry, this doesn't work for you. You should've gotten all that out before you said "I do."

Chapter 20

The Warning Signs

I've had a lot of discussions with women who have caught their men dealing with other women. Some of these examples I've even encountered myself. So these are just a few signs that your man may be talking to other women. Let's just get right to it.

- If another woman calls while you're there and he looks at the phone, sees it's her and doesn't answer. He's probably talking to her behind your back. Think about it. If it was nothing he would answer the phone in front of you.

- The next sign is if you pull up at a restaurant and he spots her car and all of sudden he decides that you should go eat somewhere else. He's talking to her because if you had not been there, he would have ate there.

- One of the most obvious signs that he's talking to someone else is if you walk up on him and he immediately gets off the phone. You already know what it is. Stop ignoring that inner conscience of yours that is constantly sending you red alerts that something is not right. It can save you a lot of heartache.

- If he talks to other women on the phone that are his so called "friends" but they only talk when you are not around. He may have something to hide.

- If he receives a number of calls from the opposite sex while you are in his presence but he doesn't answer the phone. There may be cause for concern.

- If while the two of you are out and his phone rings and he pretends to answer it, then he makes it seem like the other person hung up or their phone was breaking up. He may have something to hide.

- If he is on the phone and he turns the phone away from his ear and away from you so you can't tell the name on the screen. He may have something to hide.

- If he has a lock on his phone whenever you are around. He may have something to hide.

- If you walk in on him on the phone and he starts acting crazy by saying the same thing over and over and stuttering. Something is up.

- If when he gets text messages, he has his phone programmed not to light up for you to see who or what it is. Unless he is in the CIA there is no reason why his phone should be blacked out.

- If he disguises names in his phone, he has something to hide because if it were all so innocent there would be no reason to change names.

- Lastly. If he comes home with his clothes smelling like he took a bath in beer. He probably has something to hide because a lot of men will pour beer on their clothes to disguise the scent of another woman. (Thanks for the tip guys.)

Women, learn how to pay attention to the warning signs because in many cases these things are right there in front of you. His friends may have even warned you. I've known several cases of women in relationships with guys that share mutual friends. Now it puts the friends in an awkward position when he's cool with both of you, but at the end of the day he's a man too, and he's not going to completely sell him out, but he also knows you are a good woman so he'll say little things to warn you about him, like "he doesn't know what he wants", or "you can't change him." What he's really saying is, look, you are too good for him, he is not going to change. Move on. You can't even see the warning signs because you have made him such a priority that you are completely oblivious to everything that's going on right in front of you. Remember it's not about you. It's about him. And men, you know when you've done something wrong because you give your woman that silly I'm guilty look and all of a sudden you become so sweet. Men I'm here to tell you that she may not say anything right away, but don't think you are off the hook because that didn't go under the rug. That's why you try to change the subject, saying the same thing you already said over and over. You are not slick and we are not as dumb as you think.

For attractive lips, speak words of kindness
For beautiful eyes, seek out the good in other
people
To improve your ears, listen to the word of
God…
Author Unknown

Chapter 21

What if We Did It to You

What would happen if we acted like a man and thought like a man?

What if we cheated all the time? Would you not call us ho's?

What if we told different men everything they wanted to hear just to lead them on? Would we be inconsiderate?

What if we complimented other men while you weren't around? Would we be players?

What if we left you at home to watch the kids while we went out and did our own thing?

What if we constantly made promises that we didn't keep?

What if we gave ourselves to different men and made each one of them feel like they were the only one?

What if we said we were on the way and showed up hours later or didn't show up at all?

What if we said that the other guy was just a friend knowing he was more?

What if we lied constantly and could not be trusted out of your sight?

What if we spent money on another man that we didn't spend on you?

What if we had different men calling our phone all the time?

What if we brought different men around your child and didn't think anything of it?

What if we were as selfish as you?

What if you saw us with another man?

What if we had sex with men that you knew?

What if the shoe was on the other foot?

Chapter 22

"The Other Woman"

I got to talk to the ladies who have established themselves as being the woman on the side. First of all, there is nothing cute about hounding after another woman's man. Have the courage to go get a man of your own and stop acting like a bunch of desperados. Why are you trying to live another woman's life when you can go get your own because I guarantee you, it would be a problem if another woman tried to get a piece of your pie.

I used to spend a lot of wasted time and energy disliking these chicks because I let the devil get inside me. I came to realize that the unnecessary drama was weighing me down so I let that foolishness go. Easier said than done I know, but I had to do a "spiritual cleansing" for this situation as well. I was able to forgive my enemies and learn to love them. Be the better person and turn it over to the Lord and I guarantee that He will move those types of people out of your way. I did it and it really worked for me.

These men aren't just sleeping around and cheating by themselves. There are a whole slew of women out there that play the game too. These chicks are after your man like crack heads looking for a fix. There is nothing shy about the modern day Dirty Diana's of the world.

I hear a lot of women talking about how a good man is hard to find, but truth be told, so is a good woman. By the time you eliminate the gold diggers, unavailable men chasers, prostitutes, cheaters, compulsive liars, repeat drug addicts, and stalkers, there are not as many women for you as you men may think. And that leaves us. But then, the good men are at a disadvantage because they'll be the ones to end up with one of those types of women listed above and get messed up for us to have to try and fix. What's a girl to do you say? Pray and be patient. We have to stay prayed up about this thing and get more detailed with our prayers. Expect more from God. I'm no preacher and I definitely don't have all the answers but I know the power of prayer and faith. I'm a living testimony that He hears and answers prayers. You too can have the life you deserve. But I'm here to tell you that going after men who you know are taken will not bring you happiness because one day you are going to want a man for yourself. What are you going to do when there is another woman creeping in your backyard? What are you going to do when the shoe is on the other foot?

Chapter 23

What Women Want

Men, we want honesty and respect; it's that simple. If you've done wrong and you know you've done wrong, just own up to it. As I stated earlier, we would rather hear the truth, despite your feelings about how we may react. We respect a man who is honest more than one who lies and tries to cover things up. The best advice I can give you is to be honest; it will get you a lot further than lying. Because if you don't, when she finds out – notice I said *when*, because what's done in the dark always comes to light – it will not be pretty. Don't have us trying to figure out what's going on because nine times out of ten, that female intuition has kicked into third gear and she already knows something's up. Now it's just a matter of time before she figures it out or it comes out some other way. But if you are honest and up front, you can save yourself a lot of drama. Sure, she may be upset, but it'll be way better than her catching you in a lie. Trust me. That's how people snap and someone gets hurt and in some cases, killed.

Chapter 24

What Real Men Want

My ex fiancé told me once that a good man wants a good woman by his side who won't run when times get hard. A real woman stands by her man through thick and thin and she won't give up on her relationship when things aren't working out. I now understand where he was coming from. When my dad first got sick in 2004, my mom was there to take care of everything he needed. He went through surgery in 2005, and in 2006, he was diagnosed with cancer again. On April 15th, 2008, my dad died, and there wasn't a single day that went by that my mom was not there by his side and not one time did she complain. I mean, I never heard my mom complain about helping take care of her husband. And there were times when it got so bad that even I couldn't watch because it was too painful for my eyes to see, but she was right there. She got up every two hours in the middle of the night to give him his tube feedings and his pain medication and she cared for him every single day until the Lord called him home.

I remember one day, I told my mom, "Why don't you take a break or take a night off and get you some rest?"

And she said, "I'm fine. When I took those vows, I said 'for better or for worse' and I meant that." It was at that moment, years later, that I truly understood what my ex's statement really meant. My mom knows the true meaning of 'for better or for worse'. There are so many marriages ending in divorce because people just don't have staying power. You let finances and outside influences – all the things that the devil has created – bring your marriage down. You let them get in the way and you give up. I learned a lot from watching my parents growing up. My father took care of the bills. He was the provider, and my mother made sure that when he got home from work, he had food to eat. I never saw my dad be disrespectful to my mother in any way, nor did he let anyone else disrespect her. I always looked up to my dad and I told myself that one day, I was going to find a man to treat me the way my dad treated my mom and that I would be good to him the way my mother was for Daddy.

Chapter 25

It's Too Late, She's Gone

What these so-called playboys don't realize is that a woman is not going to play the fool for too long. One day, she's going to wake up and decide you are not worth her time anymore. Let's just hope it doesn't take years. You can step on her heart ten times and she'll take you back, but one day, she's going to get to the point when she doesn't care one way or the other and there would be nothing you could say or do to hurt her because she's not going to care, and when she gets to that point, she's gone. And don't let her get a glimpse of a better man, one who will treat her right and who knows her worth. You can forget it then.

During a recent conversation amongst us girls, we were talking about how some men really turn their game up when they feel like you are getting away from them, and the analogy my sister used is to look at it like catching a fish. The more you try to reel the fish in, the more he tries to get away. And that's what some of these men do. The more you try to move on and get away from him, the faster he tries to reel you back. It's not until you start moving in the opposite direction that he really has to put in work to catch you. He'll pull out every trick in the book just to get you back, trying to convince you that things are going to be different this time. He's so busy trying to get you back that he doesn't realize that the line has popped and you are long gone.

Chapter 26

When it's God-sent

Everyone should know by now that your blessings won't always come when you want them, but you have to continue to pray. Just because it doesn't work out for you now does not mean that it's never meant to be. It just may not be right now because if it's truly meant to be, the Lord will bring you together. Just know that the Lord is not the only one who's listening. As my sister once told me, the devil hears your prayers as well, and he also knows your wants. The devil will dangle something he knows you want in your face just to tease you with it and it only lasts for a season, but when it's God-sent, there are no games, no complicated Algebra; it's real. I believe in reading the bible and striving to be more Christ-like, but no one can honestly say that nowadays, it isn't the norm for people to get divorced. I know exactly why so many marriages are failing. There are plenty of people getting married off of the tease of the devil, whether it be a strong physical attraction, a sense of financial security, the idea of being married, doing it for the kids, or whatever the different reasons may be, but these unions are very seldom God-sent. If we would stop trying to pick our soul mates based on our own expectations and let the Lord send our soul mates to us, then I believe we would see more successful marriages. There are too many people getting married for the wrong reasons. Out of all the reasons I have heard from people I know who have gotten married, very few have said it was because they were so in love and knew without a doubt that their spouse was the only person they wanted to spend the rest of their life with.

Chapter 27

Who's Really to Blame?

Have you ever been with a man that no matter what happens or what he does wrong, he always turns it around and tries to blame it on you? Well I have and the only thing I can tell you about this type of man is that he is not ready for a serious relationship of any kind. First of all, he's too wrapped up in himself to ever be the man you need him to be. He's got some issues within that he needs to resolve before he can fully commit himself to you. You could catch him cheating and he'll still find an excuse to turn it around on you. It's your fault he cheated. It's your fault he told those lies. It's you fault he flirted with all those other women. It will also be your fault when it's finally over and that's ok. Take all the blame and walk away holding your head up. Listen to Chrisette Michele's "Blame It on Me" and keep it moving!

Chapter 28

My Mr. BIG

I'm a huge *Sex and The City* fan, and just in case you've never seen the show or the movie, it's based on four single friends, all over the age of 30, who live in New York. The show takes you through the many trials and failures of the relationships each one of them go through over a period of ten years. I consider myself the 'Carrie' of the show because my life and Carrie's have so many similarities. That wasn't just your average TV show. It was real; it was personal. Carrie is the writer who has been on and off with her longtime boyfriend, Mr. Big, over this ten-year period. And the thing that I learned from this show is that a lot of women have experienced a 'Mr. Big' at some point in their lives. Now, whether you end up married to him or not is a completely different subject, but the concept of naming him Mr. Big, to me, is that it was that big relationship with that man that you couldn't quite let go. Carrie and Big broke up more times than the law should allow, and you would think that after ten years, they both would have moved on with their lives, but fate didn't see it that way. There are a lot of women who still have a Mr. Big in their lives, and they just don't know how to let him go. No matter how many times you breakup to makeup, you can't ever really let him go. The sad thing about it is that he knows the hold he has on you. He always seems to call right when you have convinced yourself that you are finally over him.

He's the one you breakup with just to makeup with over and over again. And even when you try to convince yourself that he's not the one and that you will not go back, you always find yourselves back together. It's like there's this force, this magnet, that keeps pulling you back in. And why is that this magnet seems to get stronger when you think you are finally over him? The devil is so busy; he knows what your weaknesses are and he uses them to drain all the power you thought you had out of your body. I have watched the *Sex and the City Movie* at least 20 times, and each time I watch it, I cry at the scene when Big jilts Carrie on their wedding day. I guess it's because, deep down, I've always felt like the Big in my life would do that same thing to me. Just like Carrie and Big, we've broken up more times than the law should allow.

Unlike Carrie in the show, I didn't get with a different guy to try to get over him, because at the time, I just wasn't ready. I guess I never really moved on from Big before because I knew that if I got with someone else, no matter how good he may have been to me, it wouldn't have been enough and I would have cheated on him with Big. I swore that after one time of cheating, I would never do it again. They say that once a cheater, always a cheater, but I'm a living witness that it's not true for everyone because when it came back to me, I couldn't hardly handle it. I had enough sense to know that I wasn't going to make the same mistake twice and let karma cause me pain like that ever again.

I knew I wasn't ready to move on so I didn't bother bringing another man into my drama.

I made the ultimate sacrifice after the last breakup, though. I guess I had become numb. All the tears where gone, and it wasn't that it didn't hurt. It's just I had cried so much during all the other breakups that there were no more tears. Had he taken that ultimate sacrifice to put my mind at peace for good, I might have looked back, but he didn't, so I got up enough courage to cut the string that we were holding on by. If he asked me to marry him, I couldn't have done it, because just like Carrie and Big, I felt like he would have left me hanging. I believe that's why still, to this day, when I watch that movie, I cry during the scene when she gets out of the limo and runs up to him, crying, and starts hitting him with the flowers. She says to him, "I knew you would do this!" I remember sitting at the movies with him and I looked at him, thinking, *Would he do that to me?* And I honestly couldn't say that he wouldn't. Now, don't get me wrong; I knew he loved me. As a matter of fact, I know that he still loves me, but I don't care what anyone says – you never know everything that's going on in a man's head. You might think you know, but I promise you, you don't know everything and what you think you know can be something completely different than what he's actually thinking. It took me years of ups and downs and a baby to realize that he wasn't ready to marry me and may never be ready. So I let go of Big and walked away and for the first time, I didn't look back…